Empower Her – A Woman's Guide to Financial Independence Post Divorce

Author

Danielle A Calise

Copyright © [2024] by [Stylin' Spirit]

All rights reserved. No part of this book may be reproduced or transmitted in any form or by any means, electronic or mechanical, including photocopying, recording, or by any information storage and retrieval system, without prior written permission from the author, except for the inclusion of brief quotations in a review.

Published by [Stylin' Spirit]

www.stylin-spirit.com

First Edition: August 2024

Table of Contents

The Financial Landscape of Divorce 5

Taking Control of Your Finances 13

Budgeting for the Transition 17

Navigating Assets and Liabilities 25

Alimony and Child Support 31

Rebuilding Credit and Financial Reputation 39

Investment Strategies for the Future 45

Entrepreneurship and Career Rejuvenation 53

Protecting Your Financial Future 61

Financial Independence and Self-Care 69

Appendix 79

    Master Budget Brainstorming List 79

    From Penny Pinching to Financial Freedom: Unconventional Ways to Maximize Your Savings 97

    Credit Scores Explained: Why They Matter and How They Work 107

The Financial Landscape of Divorce

Divorce is not just an emotional and legal process; it is also a profoundly transformative and intricate financial journey. As couples decide to separate and embark on this uncharted territory, they must navigate the complexities of dividing their assets, addressing debts, and potentially paying or receiving alimony and child support. Understanding the multifaceted nature of divorce's financial implications is crucial. It not only protects you and secures your future but also equips you to transition successfully into the next chapter of your life.

One of the initial, critical steps in assessing the financial landscape of divorce is to gather all relevant financial documents. These may include bank statements, investment account statements, tax returns, property ownership documents, and any other financial records that provide a comprehensive snapshot of your financial situation. This comprehensive understanding of your financial standing will empower you in negotiations and ensure that all important details are noticed, enabling a fair and equitable resolution.

In divorce, assets become the focal point for division. These assets encompass a wide range of tangible and intangible properties, including real estate, vehicles, retirement accounts, stocks, businesses, and intellectual property, among others. Determining the value of these assets impartially is crucial to reaching a fair distribution. Engaging the expertise of a qualified appraiser or financial professional can be immensely helpful during this process, ensuring accuracy, minimizing potential disputes, and providing a solid foundation for negotiations or litigation.

When it comes to dividing real estate, aside from considering market value, it is essential to consider any outstanding mortgage or debts associated with the property. Selling the property and splitting the proceeds is a common approach, but in certain circumstances, one spouse may choose to retain the property by buying out the other spouse's share. In such situations, it is crucial to thoroughly assess your financial capacity to afford the associated costs, such as mortgage payments, property taxes, and ongoing maintenance expenses. Consulting with a mortgage specialist or financial advisor can help determine the feasibility of this decision and ensure long-term financial stability.

Sorting out the division of retirement accounts, such as 401(k)s or pension plans, can introduce complex challenges. This is where the expertise of a qualified financial planner or attorney specializing in divorce becomes crucial. They can guide you in determining the best course of action, whether it's dividing the account or rolling over funds into individual retirement accounts (IRAs) without triggering tax penalties or disrupting long-term financial goals.

Similarly, whether owned individually or jointly, businesses can present additional complications during divorce proceedings. Valuing a business requires a comprehensive assessment of its assets, liabilities, revenue, and goodwill. Goodwill, in this context, refers to the intangible value of a business, often associated with its reputation, customer base, and brand recognition. This comprehensive valuation often necessitates the involvement of a forensic accountant or business appraiser. These professionals play a crucial role in conducting a thorough valuation, mainly when a spouse has been more actively involved in the day-to-day operations or significantly contributed to the business's growth. By obtaining a fair and accurate valuation, the division of business assets can be handled smoothly, preserving the financial interests of both parties involved.

Debts, often intertwined with marital assets, emerge as another significant aspect within the financial landscape of divorce. Identifying and addressing joint debts, such as mortgages, loans, credit card balances, and outstanding bills, is essential. Effective communication with your ex-spouse and respective attorneys is paramount. It helps in determining who will be responsible for which debts and ensures an equitable distribution of financial obligations. This level of communication and control will help lay a foundation for financial stability and independence post-divorce.

One of the most complex and contentious issues in divorce is the determination of alimony and child support. Alimony, also known as spousal support, is financial assistance from one spouse to the other following divorce. Child support, on the other hand, involves financial aid paid by the non-custodial parent to support the needs of the children. Calculating and determining alimony and child support can vary based on factors such as income, earning potential, custody arrangement, and the standard of living during the marriage. Seeking guidance from an attorney or mediator specializing in family law will enable you to understand better your rights, obligations, and options to achieve a fair and reasonable outcome.

While navigating the financial landscape of divorce, it is critical to consider the long-term implications of your decisions. Rebuilding your credit and financial reputation should be a priority. Establishing individual accounts, paying bills on time, and monitoring your credit report can improve your financial standing and open up future opportunities. Actively working on financial recovery will also facilitate your ability to secure loans, purchase new assets, or start new ventures.

Investment strategies play a vital role in securing your financial future post-divorce. Reviewing and potentially adjusting your investment portfolios becomes necessary to ensure that you have a sound and diversified financial plan in line with your new circumstances. Seeking advice from a trusted financial advisor who can guide you in making informed investment decisions, managing risks, and optimizing returns will go a long way in stabilizing and enhancing your long-term financial well-being.

Entrepreneurship or career rejuvenation can be an exciting avenue for those looking to start afresh after divorce. Starting a new business or pursuing new professional opportunities can help you regain financial independence, boost self-confidence, and provide a fresh start. Assessing your skills, interests, and market demands is essential to determine the best path for your personal and financial growth. Engaging in professional development courses, seeking mentoring, or collaborating with career coaches may help navigate this transitional phase successfully.

Creating and adhering to a realistic budget is paramount as it lets you clearly understand your income, expenses, and financial goals. A well-crafted budget is a tool that will enable you to assess your financial health, determine if your current income is sufficient to cover your expenses and make adjustments as necessary. Understanding your cash flow regularly will help you make informed decisions about allocating your resources, prioritizing expenses, and planning for the future. Budgeting also allows you to identify areas where cost savings can be achieved, enabling you to build financial resilience and achieve your longer-term objectives more efficiently.

Protecting your financial future is paramount throughout and beyond the divorce process. This involves reviewing and updating your estate plan to reflect your new circumstances, ensuring that your assets are distributed according to your wishes, and securing the financial well-being of your beneficiaries. Additionally, considering insurance policies such as life insurance and disability insurance can provide an extra layer of financial security for yourself and your dependents, particularly if you have children or financial obligations that need to be met in the event of unforeseen circumstances.

While navigating the financial complexities of divorce can feel overwhelming, approaching it with a comprehensive plan and professional guidance can enable you to emerge stronger and more financially secure. By understanding the intricacies of asset division, debt management, alimony and child support, investments, career choices, budgeting, and long-term financial protection, you can lay the foundation for a stable and prosperous future. The journey may be challenging, but with careful planning and a strategic mindset, you can successfully transition into your next chapter, enabling financial independence, personal growth, and a bright future.

Taking Control of Your Finances

Amid a divorce, one of the most important aspects to regain control over is your finances. It can be daunting, but with the right plan and mindset, you can successfully navigate this challenging period and set yourself up for a secure financial future.

The first step is to gather all relevant financial information. This includes collecting copies of bank statements, tax returns, investment accounts, credit card statements, and other pertinent documents. Understanding your financial situation will help you make informed decisions and create a solid financial plan. Take the time to review your income sources and identify any potential changes in the foreseeable future. Evaluate your assets and liabilities and seek professional advice to ensure you have a comprehensive view of your financial standing.

Next, it's important to establish a new budget. Divorce often leads to a significant change in financial circumstances, so it's crucial to reassess your income and expenses. Start by listing all income sources, whether from your job, alimony, child support, or any other sources. Then, analyze your expenses and categorize them into essentials, such as housing and utilities, and discretionary items, such as dining out and entertainment. Creating a realistic budget allows you to manage your money better and meet your needs.

Reviewing your expenses, you must identify areas where you can cut back. This could involve adjusting your lifestyle, such as downsizing your home or reducing discretionary spending. It may be challenging initially, but remember that these sacrifices are temporary and will help you regain control of your finances. Look for cost-saving opportunities, such as refinancing your mortgage or negotiating lower interest rates on your credit cards. Consider exploring alternative healthcare, insurance, and other utility options to find the most cost-effective solutions without compromising on quality.

Another crucial aspect of controlling your finances during a divorce is seeking professional advice. Consulting with a financial advisor or divorce financial planner can provide valuable insights and help you make informed decisions about your money. They can assist you in understanding the tax implications of your financial settlement, managing your investments, and creating a long-term financial plan. A professional can also guide you through the complexities of dividing assets and debts, ensuring a fair and equitable distribution.

During this process, it's important to prioritize your financial well-being and take steps to protect your assets. This might involve changing passwords on financial accounts, closing joint accounts, and updating beneficiaries on insurance policies and retirement accounts. Taking proactive measures minimizes the risk of financial setbacks and lays the groundwork for a secure future. Seek legal advice to ensure you take all the necessary legal steps to protect your financial interests.

Additionally, educate yourself about the financial implications of divorce. Understand the different types of assets and how they are divided during a divorce, such as marital property, separate property, and community property. Familiarize yourself with the potential tax consequences of selling or dividing various assets. By becoming knowledgeable about these matters, you can actively participate in important financial discussions and ensure your interests are well-represented.

Lastly, taking care of yourself during this challenging time is crucial. Divorce can be emotionally and mentally draining, but nurturing your well-being will help you stay strong and focused on regaining control of your finances. Practice self-care, seek support from friends and family, and consider professional counseling. A clear and resilient mindset will support your financial journey as you move forward.

Taking control of your finances during a divorce may seem overwhelming, but remember you have the strength and resilience to come out on top. You can successfully regain control of your financial future by gathering information, creating a new budget, seeking professional advice, protecting your assets, educating yourself about the financial implications, and taking care of yourself. Remember, this is just a chapter in your life, and with careful planning, you can build a bright and secure financial future beyond divorce. Stay focused on your goals, be adaptable to changes, and stay positive even in the face of challenges, for a brighter financial future awaits you.

Budgeting for the Transition

As you navigate through the challenging divorce process, it is crucial to take control of your finances and develop a budget that will help you transition smoothly into this new phase of your life. Budgeting for the transition requires careful planning and consideration to ensure that your financial resources are effectively allocated and that you can maintain stability amid significant change.

1. Assess Your Current Financial Situation: Before creating a budget, it is essential to have a clear understanding of your current financial position. Start by gathering all relevant financial documents, such as bank statements, credit card statements, and bills. Take note of your income, expenses, and any outstanding debts or financial obligations. This comprehensive assessment will serve as the foundation for creating an effective budget.

Consider your income sources, including salary, dividends, rental income, or regular cash inflow. Evaluate the stability of your income and any potential changes that may occur in the near future, such as a change in employment or alimony payments. Assessing your income accurately will help you establish a realistic budget that reflects your financial capabilities.

Next, examine your expenses in detail. Categorize them into essential and discretionary expenses. Essential expenses typically include housing costs (mortgage or rent payments), utilities, groceries, transportation, healthcare, and childcare, if applicable. Discretionary expenses encompass entertainment, dining out, travel, hobbies, and non-essential subscriptions. By differentiating between the two, you can better understand how your money is being spent and make informed decisions about what can be adjusted or reduced.

Additionally, it is essential to identify any outstanding debts, such as credit card balances, personal loans, or student loans, and evaluate their impact on your finances. Understanding the interest rates, repayment terms, and minimum monthly payments will help you effectively determine how to allocate your budget for debt repayment.

2. Set Realistic and Attainable Goals: As you move forward with your new life, it is important to establish realistic and attainable goals. Consider both short-term and long-term objectives, such as paying off debts, saving for emergencies, rebuilding your credit, and planning for retirement. By setting specific goals, you can create a budget that aligns with these objectives and helps you make progress toward financial stability.

You may need to make some sacrifices and difficult decisions to achieve your financial goals. Assess your priorities and determine where you can cut back on expenses to redirect funds toward your goals. For example, reducing discretionary spending such as eating out or entertainment and reallocating those funds towards debt repayment or savings can significantly impact your financial well-being in the long run.

3. Analyze and Prioritize Expenses: To make informed decisions about your budget, carefully analyze your expenses. Differentiate between essential expenses, such as housing, utilities, and groceries,

and discretionary spending, such as entertainment and dining out. Prioritize your expenses based on their importance and allocate your income accordingly. This may involve making difficult decisions and cutting back on certain discretionary expenses to meet your essential needs.

To further optimize your budget, explore opportunities to cut costs and save money without sacrificing quality. Shop around for better deals on necessary services like insurance or utilities, compare prices before making big purchases, and look for ways to minimize unnecessary expenses in your daily life. Minor adjustments can add up to substantial savings over time.

Consider implementing cost-saving measures in various aspects of your life. For example, reassess your housing needs and consider downsizing or finding more affordable housing options if it makes financial sense. Look for ways to reduce energy consumption to lower utility bills. Plan your meals and grocery shopping to minimize food waste and unnecessary expenses. Explore free or low-cost entertainment options such as local community events or outdoor activities. Being mindful of your spending habits and actively seeking cost-saving opportunities will help you stretch your budget further.

4. Consider the Impact of Divorce-Related Costs: Divorce often comes with various financial costs that must be considered in your budget. These may include legal fees, mediation or counseling expenses, and potential housing or child custody arrangements changes. Make sure to factor in these costs when creating your budget, as they can significantly impact your financial situation in the short term.

Consult with your divorce attorney or financial advisor to understand the potential financial implications of your divorce settlement. Consider factors such as alimony, child support, and any property division to assess your income and expenses going forward accurately. Adjusting your budget to accommodate these new financial obligations or opportunities may be necessary.

5. Seek Professional Guidance: If you find it challenging to create a budget independently, consider seeking professional guidance from a financial advisor or budgeting expert. They can provide valuable insight, help you develop a realistic budget, and offer strategies to maximize your financial resources during this transition period.

A financial advisor can help you analyze your financial situation comprehensively, assess your goals, and provide guidance on appropriate investment strategies for your savings and retirement planning. They can also assist in optimizing your budget, exploring debt management options, and ensuring that you are on track to achieve financial stability.

6. Periodically Review and Adjust Your Budget: Creating a budget is not a one-time activity; it requires regular review and adjustment. As your circumstances change and you better understand your post-divorce financial realities, be prepared to modify your budget accordingly. Regularly reviewing and adjusting your budget will help you stay

on track and ensure that it remains relevant to your ongoing financial goals and needs.

Make it a routine to review your budget monthly or quarterly, assessing any changes in income, expenses, or financial goals. This practice will help you identify areas where you may need to adjust to better align with your financial priorities. As your financial situation improves or stabilizes post-divorce, you can also explore opportunities to allocate surplus funds towards achieving additional goals previously put on hold.

Remember, budgeting for the transition is crucial to securing your financial future after divorce. By assessing your current financial situation, setting realistic goals, prioritizing expenses, and seeking professional guidance, you can establish a budget that empowers you to regain control over your financial life and pave the way for a brighter future. With careful planning and diligence, you can build a solid financial foundation supporting your journey towards post-divorce success.

Navigating Assets and Liabilities

Navigating Assets and Liabilities:

Divorce can profoundly impact your finances, affecting your present financial situation and your long-term financial security. As you divide assets and liabilities, you must arm yourself with comprehensive knowledge and understanding. This chapter will delve deeper into the intricacies of asset and liability division, outlining key considerations and strategies to ensure a fair and equitable settlement.

To begin with, let's delve further into assets and liabilities. Assets encompass a wide range of items, including, but not limited to, real estate properties, vehicles, investment portfolios, retirement accounts, personal belongings, and even intellectual property rights. It is essential to accurately determine each asset's current value, considering both market value and sentimental attachment. Obtain professional appraisals, if necessary, to ensure a reliable valuation.

Real estate properties are often a significant asset in a divorce. Assess the current market value of any jointly-owned properties and consider the potential tax implications, maintenance costs, and future value projections when deciding whether to retain or sell the property. If one spouse wishes to keep the marital home, independently assess their ability to afford mortgage payments, property taxes, insurance, and maintenance costs. Consult a mortgage professional to understand the feasibility of refinancing the mortgage in one spouse's name.

Retirement accounts are another crucial consideration. Evaluate the balances and projected growth of individual retirement accounts (IRAs) and employer-sponsored retirement plans, such as 401(k)s or pensions. Determine the potential value disparity between the accounts due to differences in contributions or market performance. Consult a tax professional to understand the tax implications of dividing retirement accounts and explore options such as a qualified domestic relations order (QDRO) to transfer funds between accounts without incurring taxes or penalties.

Investment portfolios should also be carefully evaluated, including stocks, bonds, mutual funds, and other financial instruments. Consider the current market value, cost basis (the original purchase price), and potential capital gains or losses associated with liquidating the assets. Consult with a financial advisor or tax professional to assess the tax implications and potential investment strategies.

While often sentimental, personal belongings can also have financial implications. Consider the fair market value of valuable assets such as jewelry, art, collectibles, and antiques. If there are specific items of sentimental value, discuss potential trade-offs with other assets or consider a buyout arrangement to ensure a fair and equitable distribution.

Intellectual property rights can also be valuable assets worth considering. This can include copyrights, patents, trademarks, or royalties from creative works or business ventures. Consult an intellectual property attorney to understand these assets' potential value and future income streams.

On the other hand, liabilities encompass all outstanding debts and financial obligations. This includes mortgages, car loans, credit card debt, student loans, personal loans, tax debt, and other forms of debt incurred during the marriage. Make a comprehensive list of all outstanding liabilities, specifying the respective balances, interest rates, and payment terms to understand their impact on future financial decisions.

When determining the division of assets and liabilities, understand that the legal framework may vary across jurisdictions. Some regions adopt community property laws, which generally mandate equal division of assets and liabilities acquired during the marriage. Other jurisdictions follow equitable distribution principles, focusing on a fair allocation of assets and liabilities based on factors such as each spouse's financial circumstances, contributions to the marriage, and future earning potential.

To navigate this complex landscape, it is advisable to consult with a qualified divorce attorney specializing in family law and having expertise in financial matters. Their guidance will help you understand the laws and regulations specific to your jurisdiction, ensuring your rights and interests are protected during the asset and liability division process.

Apart from legal expertise, enlisting the services of a financial planner or advisor can provide valuable assistance. A financial professional can help you analyze the long-term consequences of various asset division scenarios and strategize their impact on your financial goals. They can offer objective advice on the potential tax implications, investment options, and overall financial planning after the divorce.

In many instances, achieving an equitable distribution of assets and liabilities involves making difficult decisions. Some assets may hold sentimental value, while others may have more substantial financial implications. Prioritize your financial goals and consider the long-term benefits and consequences of retaining or relinquishing certain assets.

When it comes to joint liabilities, creating a plan for their division is crucial. Open communication with your ex-spouse is vital to determining how best to manage these debts, including options like refinancing, debt consolidation, or outright repayment: document agreements and any financial arrangements to ensure clarity and limit potential disputes in the future.

Updating your estate planning documents is an often overlooked but essential step. Review your will, power of attorney, and beneficiary designations to align them with your new financial circumstances and distribution goals. By doing so, you are safeguarding your assets and ensuring that your wishes are honored in the event of unforeseen circumstances.

Managing the financial aftermath of a divorce can be complex and emotionally challenging. Seeking professional guidance through this process will give you the knowledge and support necessary to make informed decisions. Remember to prioritize your long-term financial well-being and establish a solid foundation for your future financial security.

Alimony and Child Support

Divorce is both an emotional and personal journey and a financial one. Alimony and child support are vital in ensuring financial stability for both parties involved. These financial arrangements can have a profound and lasting impact on the lives of individuals and their children.

Alimony, also known as spousal support or maintenance, is a form of financial assistance provided by one spouse to the other after a divorce. Its purpose is to help the lower-earning or non-earning spouse maintain a similar standard of living as they had during the marriage. The amount and duration of alimony vary depending on various factors, including the length of the marriage, the income and earning potential of both spouses, the age and health of each party, and the financial needs of both individuals.

Gathering all necessary financial information is crucial to establish an appropriate alimony amount. This process includes income statements, tax returns, and documentation of expenses. Each party should disclose their financial situation wholly and honestly. Consulting with a financial advisor or attorney specializing in divorce can be immensely helpful in navigating the complex process of calculating alimony.

Different states have different approaches to determining alimony, and various alimony arrangements exist. Understanding the nuances of each type is essential for making informed decisions:

1. Temporary or rehabilitative alimony: This type of alimony is awarded for a specific period and aims to support the receiving spouse. At the same time, the receiving spouse gains education, training, or employment skills to become self-supporting. This could involve acquiring new qualifications, obtaining job experience, or completing a professional development program. The primary goal is enabling the receiving spouse to achieve financial independence.

2. Permanent alimony: As the name suggests, this form of alimony is ongoing and continues indefinitely until the

receiving spouse remarries, or either party passes away. Permanent alimony is typically awarded in cases where one spouse has a significant financial disadvantage due to factors such as age, health, or long-term responsibilities, making it difficult to achieve financial independence. It is usually seen in long-term marriages where one spouse significantly contributes to the household while the other focuses on personal pursuits or career development.

3. Lump-sum alimony: In some instances, the parties may agree to a one-time payment or a series of payments instead of ongoing monthly payments. This can provide a clean break and prevent future financial entanglement. Lump-sum alimony is attractive when both parties desire a clean and final separation.

4. Reimbursement alimony: This alimony is awarded to reimburse one spouse for contributing to the other spouse's education, training, or career development during the marriage. It is often granted when one spouse supports

the other financially while they pursue their professional goals. Reimbursement alimony recognizes the sacrifices made by one spouse to support and facilitate the other's advancement, ensuring fairness and acknowledging their contributions.

On the other hand, child support is specifically designated to cover the expenses related to raising children after divorce. The primary custodial parent usually receives child support payments on behalf of the children to ensure their financial well-being and stability. The amount of child support is determined using guidelines provided by the state, which consider factors such as the parents' incomes, the number of children, and the children's needs.

Child support is crucial for meeting a child's basic needs, including food, clothing, education, medical expenses, and extracurricular activities. It is essential to approach child support discussions with a focus on the child's best interests and to ensure that adequate financial provisions are made to support their upbringing. Both parents have a legal responsibility to contribute to the financial welfare of their children.

It is important to note that alimony and child support are separate concepts, each with specific considerations. While child support is usually calculated using specific guidelines, alimony is more subjective and can be negotiated between the parties involved. However, certain states have established formulas for determining alimony and child support, adding more consistency to the process.

Negotiating alimony and child support can be challenging and emotionally charged. It is essential to approach these discussions clearly and understand your financial needs and obligations. Aim for fair and reasonable outcomes, prioritizing the well-being of all parties involved, especially children affected by the divorce.

When considering alimony and child support, exploring the long-term financial implications is wise. Create a budget that takes into account these support payments, as they will impact your overall financial situation. In some cases, adjustments and sacrifices may be necessary to maintain a stable financial future for both parties involved. Consider speaking with a financial advisor specializing in divorce proceedings to understand better how alimony and child support will impact your financial outlook.

In addition to financial support, it is crucial to address the issue of healthcare coverage for both the receiving spouse and children. The divorcing couple should determine who will provide healthcare coverage and how the associated costs will be managed.

Sometimes, the paying spouse may also be required to obtain life insurance policies to secure their financial responsibilities. This protects the receiving spouse and children if the paying spouse passes away, ensuring that financial support continues uninterrupted.

Remember that alimony and child support arrangements are not set in stone. As circumstances change, such as job loss or a significant increase in income, it may be necessary to modify these arrangements through the appropriate legal processes. Always consult with an attorney or mediator before making any changes to ensure compliance with the law.

Both parties must enter divorce proceedings with a knowledgeable and strategic approach to alimony and child support. Seek professional advice, gather the necessary financial information, and focus on creating a fair and sustainable support structure that prioritizes the well-being of everyone affected by the divorce. With careful consideration and diligence, the financial aspects of divorce can be navigated with confidence, ensuring a solid foundation for the future.

Rebuilding Credit and Financial Reputation

Rebuilding Credit and Financial Reputation

Rebuilding your credit and financial reputation becomes critical on your journey toward financial independence after a divorce. Divorce can often wreak havoc on your credit score and financial standing, but with the right strategies and commitment, you can take control and start rebuilding.

The first step in this process is to assess the damage to your credit thoroughly. It is crucial to obtain a copy of your credit report from all three major credit bureaus—Equifax, Experian, and TransUnion. By carefully reviewing each report, you can identify errors, inaccuracies, or any accounts that may have been overlooked during the divorce process.

Once you understand your credit situation, it's time to create a detailed improvement plan. While there is no quick fix for rebuilding credit, implementing several key steps can help you rebuild your credit and regain your financial reputation over time.

1. Paying your bills on time is crucial for rebuilding your credit. Your payment history is a major factor in determining your credit score, so making timely payments on all of your bills is crucial for demonstrating your financial responsibility. Consider setting up automatic bill payments, scheduling payment reminders, or utilizing budgeting tools to avoid missing due dates. Implementing these strategies will not only rebuild your payment history but also instill discipline in managing your finances.

2. Reducing your debt is another essential aspect of rebuilding your credit. High debt levels can weigh heavily on your credit score and hinder your ability to regain financial stability. Creating a debt repayment plan will help you regain control of your finances. Start by prioritizing your debts and focusing on paying off high-interest debts first. This approach saves money in interest payments and reduces the overall financial burden. You can also consider

debt consolidation options, negotiating with creditors to lower interest rates, or creating a manageable payment plan that aligns with your financial situation.

3. Using credit responsibly is vital in the process of rebuilding credit. While it may be tempting to avoid credit altogether after experiencing financial challenges, rebuilding your credit requires responsible credit usage. Start by applying for a secured credit card or becoming an authorized user on someone else's account. Use the card sparingly and make timely payments to demonstrate your ability to manage credit responsibly. It's important not to overextend yourself and only take on as much credit as you can comfortably manage. This responsible credit usage will slowly rebuild your creditworthiness and establish a positive credit history.

4. Building a positive credit history is crucial in rebuilding your financial standing. If your credit was severely impacted during the divorce, you may need help obtaining new credit. However, there are still

options available. Consider opening new credit accounts, such as a small personal loan or a low-limit credit card, and make regular payments on these accounts. Doing so shows potential lenders that you can manage credit responsibly and can be trusted. Be cautious to take on only a little credit at once, as it may become overwhelming. Only borrow what you can afford to repay to ensure a sustainable financial recovery.

5. Monitoring your credit regularly is essential as you progress to rebuild your credit and financial reputation. Periodically check your credit reports for errors, inconsistencies, or any accounts that may still impact your credit. By monitoring your credit regularly, you can address any issues promptly and ensure your credit information is accurate. It's crucial to set up free credit monitoring services, access your credit reports through annualcreditreport.com, or consider subscribing to a credit monitoring service for additional protection and real-time alerts.

Monitoring your credit allows you to stay proactive and take immediate action if negative information appears on your report.

6. In certain situations, seeking professional help can be beneficial in rebuilding credit. If you find it difficult to navigate on your own or face significant challenges in your credit repair journey, consider contacting a credit counseling agency or a financial advisor. These professionals specialize in credit repair and can offer guidance, negotiate with creditors on your behalf, and provide personalized strategies to help you rebuild your credit effectively. However, it's important to choose reputable professionals who have your best interests at heart. Research their credentials and seek recommendations before engaging in their services.

Rebuilding credit and financial reputation after a divorce can be daunting, but with patience, perseverance, and consistent effort, it is possible to regain financial stability. Remember to focus on your long-term financial goals and not let setbacks discourage you. Taking control of your credit and financial situation will pave the way for a brighter future and open doors to new opportunities. Your commitment to rebuilding your credit will not only rebuild your financial reputation but also provide a solid foundation for a successful and secure financial future.

Investment Strategies for the Future

Investment Strategies for the Future

Amid a divorce, it is crucial to start planning for your financial future, as this will play a significant role in your overall well-being and stability. One key element of this plan is implementing investment strategies that will help you grow and protect your assets. By taking a comprehensive approach and considering various factors, you can make informed decisions that align with your goals and financial situation.

1. Assess Your Risk Tolerance: Before diving into specific investment options, it is important to understand your risk tolerance. Risk tolerance refers to your ability to handle fluctuations in the value of your investments and your comfort level with potential losses. Evaluating your risk tolerance will help you determine the appropriate investments. This assessment is crucial because it sets the foundation for your investment strategy and enables you to find the right balance between risk and reward.

Understanding risk tolerance involves considering your financial goals, time horizon, financial obligations, and emotional resilience. If you have a longer time horizon and can tolerate short-term market fluctuations, you may opt for investments with higher potential returns, such as stocks. On the other hand, if your focus is capital preservation and stability, you may lean towards more conservative investments like bonds or real estate.

2. Set Clear Financial Goals: Establishing clear financial goals is essential for designing an effective investment strategy. These goals include saving for retirement, funding your children's education, purchasing a new home, or simply growing your wealth. Take the time to define your objectives clearly, both in terms of short-term milestones and long-term aspirations. This exercise will guide your investment decisions and enable you to allocate your resources effectively.

Not all goals have the same time horizon and risk requirements. Retirement, for example, is a long-term goal that may involve a more aggressive investment approach. However, saving for a down payment on a home may require a more conservative strategy due to the shorter time horizon. Be specific about your goals and ensure they are realistic and achievable. This will provide a roadmap for investment decisions and help you evaluate your progress.

3. Diversify Your Portfolio: Diversification is a key concept in investment strategy. It involves spreading your investments across different assets, such as stocks, bonds, real estate, and mutual funds. By diversifying your portfolio, you can mitigate risk and maximize returns. Remember that different investments tend to perform differently under various market conditions. Therefore, a well-diversified portfolio can help cushion the impact of market volatility. Consider seeking advice from a financial advisor to help you create a diversified portfolio tailored to your goals and risk tolerance.

Diversification extends beyond asset classes and involves diversifying within each asset class. For example, you may opt for a diversified portfolio of stocks from different sectors and industries instead of owning a few individual stocks. Additionally, diversifying geographically can reduce exposure to any region's economic or political risks. Remember that diversification does not guarantee profits or protect against losses but can help manage risk in your investment portfolio.

4. Invest for the Long Term: Focusing on immediate financial needs and reacting to short-term market fluctuations is tempting in a divorce situation. However, it is crucial to maintain a long-term perspective on investing. Investing for the long term allows you to ride out market volatility and benefit from compounding, which is the exponential growth of your investments over time. Avoid making impulsive decisions based on unsettling market news or short-term trends. Embrace a disciplined and patient approach, keeping your long-term goals in mind.

Long-term investing focuses on the fundamental strengths and growth prospects of your investments. It requires patience and the ability to withstand short-term market fluctuations. By staying invested over the long term, you can take advantage of the power of compounding, where your investment returns generate additional returns, thus accelerating your wealth accumulation. Revisiting and rebalancing your portfolio periodically, instead of frequently trying to time the market, is the key to successful long-term investing.

5. Consider Tax-Efficient Investments: Taxes can significantly impact your investment returns. Therefore, it is wise to consider tax-efficient investment vehicles that can help you grow your wealth more effectively. For example, tax-deferred retirement accounts like Individual Retirement Accounts (IRAs) or employer-sponsored 401(k) plans offer tax advantages that can minimize your tax liability in the long run. Another option is tax-efficient index funds or exchange-traded funds (ETFs) that generate fewer taxable events. Consult with a financial advisor or tax professional to evaluate tax-efficient strategies based on your circumstances.

In addition to tax-advantaged accounts, tax-loss harvesting is another strategy to consider. By strategically selling decreased-value investments, you can generate capital losses that may offset capital gains and reduce your taxable income. However, it is crucial to familiarize yourself with the tax rules and guidelines to avoid potential pitfalls or violations.

6. Stay Informed and Educated: Investing is a continuously evolving field, and staying informed about market trends and investment opportunities is crucial. Allocate time to enhance your investment knowledge through various resources. Follow reputable financial news outlets, read books by renowned investors, attend webinars, and consider joining investment clubs or forums where you can exchange ideas with like-minded individuals. Remember that education is empowering and can help you make informed investment decisions.

Investing may seem complex, but continuous learning and staying up-to-date with market developments can help you develop a solid understanding of investment principles and strategies. This knowledge will aid you in making informed investment decisions and enable you to participate more actively in discussions with your financial advisor or other investment professionals.

7. Regularly Reassess and Adjust: As your financial situation and goals may evolve, it is important to reassess and adjust your investment strategy accordingly. Life events, such as changes in employment, remarriage, or childbirth, may impact your financial goals and risk tolerance. Schedule periodic reviews with your financial advisor to ensure your investments align with your objectives and make any necessary adjustments.

Reassessment should also consider changes in market conditions or the economic outlook. For instance, if market performance significantly deviates from your expected returns or there are significant shifts in the global or local economy, you may need to reassess your asset allocation or consider alternative investment opportunities. Remember that investment strategies are not set in stone and should be flexible to accommodate changing circumstances and new information.

By implementing these investment strategies and continuously assessing and adjusting them, you can work towards securing your financial independence and building a strong foundation for the years to come. As you navigate the complexities of divorce, having a well-thought-out investment plan will give you the confidence and peace of mind needed to thrive in your post-divorce financial life.

Entrepreneurship and Career Rejuvenation

In the aftermath of a divorce, when your life may feel like it's been turned upside down, it is common to seek a fresh start in your career. This is an opportune moment to explore entrepreneurship, allowing you to regain control, find fulfillment, and secure financial independence. Embracing entrepreneurship will enable you to create a life that aligns with your passions and dreams. While embarking on this journey may seem daunting, breaking it down into key considerations and taking strategic steps can pave the way for a successful entrepreneurial venture.

1. Self-reflection and goal-setting: Begin by deep self-reflection and envisioning your desired future. Take time to evaluate your passions, strengths, and long-term goals. What motivates and inspires you? What unique skills and experiences can you bring to the table? Defining your vision will serve as the compass that guides your decisions and keeps you focused on the path ahead. Create a

mission statement that encapsulates your purpose and values, reminding you why you're embarking on this entrepreneurial journey.

2. Research and market analysis: Before diving headfirst into a new venture, it is crucial to conduct comprehensive market research. Identify gaps, trends, and potential customers within your desired industry. Understand the competitive landscape and assess market demand. This research will ensure that your business idea stands on a solid foundation. Dive deep into industry reports, customer surveys, and market trends to gain valuable insights to inform your decision-making process.

3. Developing a business plan: A well-crafted business plan is a roadmap for your entrepreneurial journey. It outlines your goals, target market, products or services, marketing strategies, financial projections, etc. A business plan is a decision-making tool that can help you secure funding. Take the time to thoroughly flesh out each aspect of your

plan, ensuring it is comprehensive and realistic. Break down your goals into actionable steps, establishing timelines and metrics to measure progress.

4. Acquiring necessary skills and knowledge: Depending on your chosen field, you may need to acquire or enhance your existing skills. Explore courses, workshops, mentorship programs, or conferences to further your knowledge and proficiency. Investing in your personal and professional development will boost your confidence and equip you with the tools needed for success. Connect with industry experts, trusted advisors, or successful entrepreneurs to gain insights and learn valuable lessons from their experiences.

5. Building a support network: Entrepreneurship can be a solitary journey, but it doesn't have to be. Surround yourself with a supportive community of like-minded individuals who can offer guidance, encouragement, and networking opportunities. Join professional associations, attend industry

events, connect with other entrepreneurs, and seek mentorship connections. A strong support network will uplift you during challenging times and exponentially expand your opportunities. Collaborate with fellow entrepreneurs, form partnerships, and seek mentors who can provide advice and support as you navigate the complexities of entrepreneurship.

6. Securing financing: Starting a new business often requires capital investment. Explore various funding options, such as small business loans, grants, or crowdfunding platforms, to secure the financial resources needed to bring your venture to life. Research and understand the requirements and terms of each funding option, ensuring they align with your long-term goals. Prepare a thorough financial forecast demonstrating the viability and profitability of your business to attract potential investors or lenders.

7. Creating a marketing and branding strategy: Building a successful business

entails effectively reaching and engaging your target audience. Develop a comprehensive marketing and branding strategy to promote your products or services. Utilize social media platforms, content marketing, search engine optimization, and other digital strategies to connect with potential customers. Embrace online and offline marketing techniques, and consistently evaluate and adjust your approach based on analytics and customer feedback. Build a strong brand identity that resonates with your target audience and conveys the unique value you offer.

8. Embracing adaptability and continuous learning: Entrepreneurship is a constant learning and adaptation journey. Stay open to feedback and be willing to iterate your business strategies. Keep a keen eye on industry trends, technological advancements, and changes in customer preferences. Embrace a growth mindset that encourages personal and professional development, allowing you to stay agile and ahead of the curve.

Seek customer feedback, conduct regular market research, and adapt your business model to remain relevant and competitive.

9. Balancing work and personal life: As an entrepreneur, it is easy to get consumed by work. However, maintaining a healthy work-life balance is essential for long-term success and personal well-being. Establish boundaries, prioritize self-care, spend quality time with loved ones, and engage in activities that bring you joy. Remember that your personal life is just as valuable as your entrepreneurial pursuits. Delegate tasks, build a reliable team, and create systems and processes that promote efficiency and allow you time for work and personal pursuits.

10. Celebrate milestones and persevere: Celebrate your achievements, no matter how small, and acknowledge the milestones you reach. Entrepreneurship is challenging, but by staying determined, adaptable, and passionate, you have the potential to create a prosperous and fulfilling career. Embrace

the lessons learned from setbacks and mistakes, as they will ultimately shape your journey toward success. Surround yourself with positive affirmations, visualize your goals, and stay focused on the long-term vision. Remember that resilience and perseverance will strengthen you during tough times and contribute to your ultimate triumph.

You can redefine your career through entrepreneurship and create a life of purpose and fulfillment. Trust in your abilities, leverage your unique experiences, and face the entrepreneurial journey with resilience and dedication. By taking deliberate steps toward your goals, embracing continuous learning, and fostering a mindset of adaptability, you will unlock remarkable possibilities and discover the immense fulfillment of building a successful business on your terms.

Protecting Your Financial Future

Divorce is a deeply transformative period that affects various aspects of your life, including your financial well-being. Taking proactive measures to safeguard your financial future is crucial as you navigate the complexities of this transition. By carefully considering and implementing the following steps, you can establish a solid foundation for your financial security.

1. Review and Update Legal Documents:

As you embark on your divorce journey, reviewing and updating any legal documents that may have named your former spouse as a beneficiary or granted them, decision-making authority is essential. Seek the guidance of a knowledgeable attorney to ensure your will, power of attorney, healthcare proxies, and any other legal documents accurately represent your current wishes and life circumstances. Clarifying beneficiaries and designating trusted individuals in these documents will protect your financial interests and uphold your wishes.

Furthermore, it is important to consider updating your Social Security information. If you were married for over ten years, you may be eligible to claim Social Security benefits based on your ex-spouse's earnings record. Understanding the eligibility criteria and the potential impact on your future financial security can be complex, so consulting with a financial advisor or the Social Security Administration can provide the necessary guidance.

2. Assess Insurance Coverage:

Divorce often results in changes to your insurance coverage. Begin by evaluating your health insurance needs as you separate from your spouse's policy, considering options such as employer-provided coverage, private plans, or COBRA continuation. Comparing premiums, deductibles, and coverage limits will help you choose the most suitable situation. If you have children, address their insurance needs through child support arrangements or by exploring coverage options like Medicaid or the Children's Health Insurance Program (CHIP).

Review your life insurance policies and adjust beneficiaries and coverage amounts. Consider your long-term financial goals and the financial support you would want to provide for your loved ones in your absence. If you are receiving or paying alimony or child support, consider purchasing term life insurance to secure the financial obligations outlined in the divorce settlement.

Additionally, assess disability insurance to protect your income in the event of an unexpected illness or injury. Disability insurance can provide a portion of your salary should you become unable to work temporarily or permanently. Evaluate the policy terms, waiting periods, and benefit amounts to ensure adequate coverage that aligns with your financial goals.

3. Scrutinize the Settlement Agreement:

Dividing assets and liabilities is a key element of the divorce process. When reviewing the settlement agreement, exercise diligence and consider all financial aspects carefully. Seek the assistance of a financial advisor or attorney specializing in divorce settlements to help you understand the short—and long-term implications of various financial decisions.

Consider the valuation and division of marital property, including real estate, retirement accounts, investments, and personal belongings. Be aware of potential tax consequences associated with specific assets. For example, the division of a retirement account may trigger tax liabilities if not appropriately structured. It is crucial to evaluate the potential tax implications of each division scenario to make informed decisions that minimize your tax burden.

Pay close attention to debts and liabilities, such as mortgages, credit card balances, and loans. Determine how these obligations will be shared and ensure your name is removed from joint debts to protect your credit score. Establishing financial boundaries within the settlement agreement will help you start your post-divorce life on a solid financial footing.

4. Create a Comprehensive Financial Plan:

To protect your financial future, develop a comprehensive financial plan that meets your immediate needs while accounting for long-term goals. Start by identifying your financial priorities—retirement planning, saving for your children's education, or purchasing a home.

With clear goals, you can create a roadmap aligning with your desired outcomes.

Establishing a budget is a crucial component of your financial plan. Evaluate your income, expenses, and lifestyle changes that may impact your financial situation after divorce. Separate joint accounts, close unnecessary credit card accounts, and track your spending to ensure your budget remains achievable and aligned with your new circumstances. Consider working with a financial planner who can provide guidance tailored to your unique circumstances and assist in creating a personalized financial roadmap.

When considering long-term goals, retirement planning takes center stage. Divorce may affect your retirement savings and entitlements to Social Security benefits. Understanding your retirement income's nuances and potential impacts is crucial for making informed decisions. Explore options such as contributing to individual retirement accounts (IRAs), maximizing employer-sponsored retirement plans, or exploring alternate retirement savings vehicles to ensure a comfortable retirement.

5. Establish an Emergency Fund:

Building an emergency fund is vital to safeguarding your financial stability. Life can bring unexpected expenses or income disruptions, and having a financial safety net can mitigate stress and provide a sense of security. Aim to save three to six months' living expenses in a separate, easily accessible account.

As you rebuild your financial life, consider setting aside additional funds for specific goals such as homeownership, education, or starting a business. Differentiate between short-term and long-term savings to ensure your emergency fund remains intact while working towards achieving your aspirations.

6. Seek Professional Guidance:

Divorce is a complex financial process, and seeking professional guidance can make a significant difference in securing your financial future. Engaging the services of a financial planner or advisor specializing in divorce can offer valuable insights and expertise.

Work with professionals with experience in divorce financial planning to navigate the intricacies of dividing assets, advise you on investment strategies, and offer ongoing support as you move forward. They can analyze the settlement agreement, help you evaluate the short and long-term implications of financial decisions, and suggest ways to optimize your financial situation. Their expertise will provide confidence and clarity as you make informed decisions about your financial future.

In conclusion, protecting your financial future requires active and intentional effort. By reviewing and updating legal documents, assessing insurance coverage, scrutinizing settlement agreements, creating a comprehensive financial plan, establishing an emergency fund, and seeking professional guidance, you can lay a solid framework to build upon. Embrace this opportunity to take control of your financial destiny and pave the way for a prosperous, independent, and fulfilling future beyond divorce.

Financial Independence and Self-Care

Achieving financial independence becomes a key goal in rebuilding your life after divorce. However, it is essential to remember that financial freedom is not just about accumulating wealth; it also involves caring for yourself and finding balance in all aspects of your life. In this final chapter, we will explore the importance of self-care and how it relates to your financial well-being.

1. Prioritizing Self-Care:

    After going through a divorce, it is crucial to prioritize self-care to heal emotionally, physically, and mentally. Self-care goes beyond pampering yourself with occasional indulgences. It involves creating a holistic and intentional approach to your well-being. Start by nurturing your emotional health through therapy, counseling, or joining support groups. Healing from a divorce can be long and complex, and having a supportive network can be very beneficial.

Additionally, focusing on your physical well-being is equally important. Engage in regular exercise, eat nutritious foods, and get enough sleep. Your physical health directly impacts your mental and emotional state, and investing in healthy habits can empower you to face life's challenges with greater resilience.

Taking time for yourself also means setting aside regular breaks and engaging in enjoyable activities. It could be as simple as indulging in a hobby, reading a book, walking in nature, or even taking a relaxing bath. These moments of rejuvenation allow you to recharge and regain strength, preventing burnout and stress.

2. Cultivating a Healthy Financial Mindset:

Your mindset plays a significant role in achieving financial independence. Cultivate a positive mindset that aligns with your financial goals and values. Begin by being aware of your spending patterns and identifying unhealthy financial habits. Self-reflection is essential in this process. Understand what triggers impulsive or emotional spending and work towards building healthier alternatives.

Setting realistic financial goals is important to a healthy financial mindset. Evaluate your current financial situation and establish short-term and long-term goals that align with your values and aspirations. These goals include saving for retirement, creating an emergency fund, or paying off debts. By setting specific, measurable, achievable, relevant, and time-bound (SMART) goals, you can make a roadmap for your financial journey.

Practicing gratitude for what you already have is another way to foster a healthy financial mindset. Being content with what you have in the present moment helps you avoid unnecessary spending to fill emotional voids. Shift your focus from what you lack to what you have, and appreciate the abundance in your life. This mindset shift allows you to make wiser financial choices and understand your progress towards your goals.

It is also important to Develop financial literacy and educate yourself about managing money effectively. Take the time to learn about budgeting, investing, and understanding financial statements. This knowledge empowers you to make informed decisions and take control of your financial future.

Moreover, embrace the idea of self-worth and financial worthiness. Recognize that you deserve financial security and abundance. Release any limiting beliefs or negative self-talk that may hinder your financial well-being. Trust your ability to create and manage wealth; believe you deserve financial success.

3. Building Wealth for the Future:

As you work towards financial independence, developing a long-term wealth-building strategy is essential. This involves diversifying your investment portfolio, focusing on growing assets, and managing risks. Seek professional advice from financial advisors who can guide you in creating an investment plan based on your financial goals, risk tolerance, and time horizon.

One crucial aspect of building wealth is investing in retirement accounts. Start contributing to retirement funds early, taking advantage of employer matching programs or tax benefits. Understanding the power of compound interest and long-term investments can significantly impact your financial future. It is also important to regularly review and adjust your investment strategy as your financial situation evolves.

Additionally, consider building multiple streams of income. This can involve exploring side hustles, starting a business, or investing in income-generating assets such as rental properties or dividend-paying stocks. Generating passive income increases your financial security and provides a sense of financial freedom.

Furthermore, be mindful of managing debt effectively. Prioritize paying off high-interest debts and develop a strategy to reduce and eliminate debt over time. This includes creating a comprehensive debt repayment plan and considering debt consolidation options.

4. Prioritizing Your Happiness:

   While striving for financial independence, it is crucial not to sacrifice your well-being and happiness. Take the time to identify what truly brings you joy and fulfillment and incorporate those elements into your life. Pursue your passions and interests, spend quality time with loved ones, engage in activities that bring you inner peace, or embark on new adventures.

   Striking a balance between work and personal life is essential. Prioritize self-care activities, set boundaries, and find ways to disconnect from work-related stressors. Engage in activities that recharge your creative energies and allow you to thrive in your personal and professional pursuits.

Additionally, practice mindfulness and cultivate a positive mindset. Be present in the moment, practice gratitude, and focus on the positives in your life. This mindset shift can reduce stress and anxiety while enhancing your overall well-being.

Remember that happiness is not solely dependent on financial success. Take the time to cultivate relationships, connect with others, and contribute to your community or causes that are meaningful to you. Giving back and helping others can bring immense joy and fulfillment, regardless of your financial situation.

5. Seeking Support and Collaboration:

   Building financial independence does not mean you have to do it alone. Surround yourself with a supportive network of family, friends, and professionals who can guide and assist you. Join support groups or seek financial education resources to build knowledge and confidence. Collaboration can provide valuable insights and emotional support during your journey toward financial independence.

Reach out to financial advisors, lawyers, accountants, or mentors who can provide professional guidance tailored to your specific needs. Establishing a team of trusted advisors can ensure that you have access to expert advice and support when making critical financial decisions.

Additionally, consider collaborating with others who share similar financial goals. Form or join investment clubs, networking groups, or online communities where you can share experiences and knowledge. Collaborating with like-minded individuals can broaden your perspectives, open new opportunities, and help you stay motivated toward financial independence.

In this book, we have explored the various aspects of navigating the financial landscape of divorce and rebuilding your life. Financial independence is a crucial milestone in this journey, but it should always be coupled with self-care and a focus on overall well-being. By prioritizing self-care, cultivating a healthy financial mindset, building wealth for the future, prioritizing happiness, and seeking support, you can achieve a fulfilling and financially independent life after divorce. Remember, the road may have been challenging, but you have the strength and determination to create a bright and prosperous future for yourself.

Appendix

Master Budget Brainstorming List

Housing Costs

Mortgages or rent/lease payments:

Principal

Interest

Homeowners Insurance/renters insurance

Understanding the Components of Housing Costs

When contemplating the viability of refinancing, it's crucial to grasp the various components that constitute housing costs. Understanding these costs, particularly mortgage rates, which signify the cost of borrowing money, is key. This interest, the amount charged by the bank or lending company for using their funds, is repaid over a specific period, typically 15 to 30 years. It's important to note that the larger the personal loans and the longer the repayment period, the more you pay in interest compared to the asset's actual value.

When applying for a home loan, ensuring there are no prepayment penalties is essential. These penalties can limit your ability to make principal-only payments, which can significantly reduce the overall interest paid on the loan and shorten its duration. A smart strategy to consider is to make an extra monthly payment on your mortgage. This simple action can lead to substantial savings in the long run, providing a brighter financial future and a sense of optimism about your debt repayment.

A commonly used rule of thumb is that refinancing may be worthwhile if you can lower the mortgage rates on your home loan by at least 1%. However, it is important to note that if you are currently facing cash flow issues, extending the personal loan period may provide temporary relief, although it will ultimately increase the overall cost of financing over the loan's lifetime.

Home insurance is another important aspect to consider when it comes to housing costs. The cost of homeowners insurance is influenced by several factors, including deductibles, liability coverage, supplemental coverage for valuable items such as art or jewelry, and the expenses associated with rebuilding in the event of loss or damage. Regularly reviewing and updating these considerations annually is crucial. It ensures that you are adequately protected and not underinsured, providing a sense of security and peace of mind.

For those who rent or lease their residence, it is equally important to carefully review the rental or lease agreement to ensure that your home insurance coverage adequately protects you from potential losses. It is worth noting that the homeowner's insurance policy of the property owner typically only covers your personal possessions if explicitly stated in your agreement.

By understanding the various components of housing costs, such as mortgage rates, prepayment penalties, and home insurance coverage, you can make informed decisions about refinancing and ensure you are adequately protected financially. It's crucial to review and update these factors regularly, including the terms of your personal loans. This practice will help you stay on top of your housing costs and make the most financially sound choices for your situation.

Home equity loans or line of credit payments

Homeowners Association Dues

Sewer

Water

Landscaping maintenance

The cost of landscaping can fluctuate significantly throughout the year, depending on the climate of the area you live in. This is an important consideration when planning your landscaping project. Factors such as seasonal changes, weather conditions, and the specific needs of the plants and materials you choose can influence the expenses associated with maintaining and beautifying your outdoor space. For instance, in regions with harsh winters, you may need to invest in winterizing your garden or protecting delicate plants from frost damage. Conversely, in areas with hot and dry summers, considerations like irrigation systems or drought-resistant plants might be necessary to ensure the longevity and vitality of your landscape. By comprehending the impact of climate on landscaping costs, you can make informed decisions and create a beautiful outdoor space that thrives in your specific environment.

Pest control

Natural Gas

Propane (for rural homes)

Electricity

Cable, satellite, dish, streaming, or other subscription costs

Internet

Phone (Landline and or cell phone)

Utility providers often raise their rates periodically, influenced by long-term trends and seasonal fluctuations. If managing your monthly expenses is a concern, opting for level payments throughout the year is beneficial. Many utility companies offer this option, but you can also independently implement this strategy to manage your fixed expenses. For example, in regions with warmer climates, the cost of air conditioning tends to rise sharply during the summer months. By spreading your payments evenly over the year, you can better anticipate and manage these increased expenses, ensuring a more stable financial situation.

Home Maintenance

Having a home repair fund for potential equipment breakdowns can provide a sense of security and preparedness. This fund ensures that you are financially ready to handle unexpected home maintenance issues, reducing the stress and uncertainty that can come with these situations.

Understanding the age of your appliances, air conditioning, and furnace can provide valuable information for your savings and investment accounts. This knowledge lets you anticipate when they might require maintenance or replacement, helping you plan and budget accordingly. Furthermore, it can help you make informed decisions about energy efficiency. Older appliances and HVAC systems are often less energy-efficient than newer models, leading to higher utility bills. By knowing the age of these items, you can assess whether investing in newer, more energy-efficient alternatives is more cost-effective. This knowledge empowers you to maintain the functionality and efficiency of your household appliances, air conditioning, and furnace, saving you time, money, and potential headaches in the long run.

Home maintenance (annual furnace tune-up, lawn care, gardening, etc.)

A home upgrade/remodel fund (new appliances, painting needs, etc.)

A new furniture fund

Tax preparation and legal fees

Vehicle and Transportation Costs

Vehicle purchase payments or lease payments

Auto insurance premiums

Insurance deductibles

Fuel costs

Public transportation

Parking expenses

Establishing a vehicle maintenance fund for regular expenses like oil changes, car washes, new tires, and wiper fluid demonstrates a proactive and responsible approach to vehicle ownership. This fund ensures that you are financially prepared for these routine but necessary costs, contributing to a sense of control and stability in your transportation expenses.

Toll fees

Vehicle registration and DMV costs

A vehicle repair fund (to fund future vehicle repair costs)

Vehicle storage costs

Transportation costs specific to your commute

Parking fees

Groceries & Household Supplies

General groceries and cleaning supplies

Social/family gatherings

Holiday food funds

Eating out (including lunch for work)

First-aid supplies

Vitamins and other health supplements

Non-prescription (over-the-counter) medicines

Haircare products

Employment Related Expenses

Work clothing/uniforms

Dry cleaning expenses

Client gifts and other client expenses

Professional fees

Licensing costs (if applicable)

Continuing education costs

Work travel expenses

Coworker gifts and celebration-related expenses

Work-related social gatherings

Health and Medical

A clinic and hospital copay fund

Prescription medicines

Dental care costs

Eye care costs

Naturopathic, homeopathic, and alternative health costs

Medical equipment

Orthodontic care

Out-of-pocket deductibles

Health insurance premiums

HSA and FSA contributions

New baby/child medical expenses

Annual Checkups and Copays

Personal Care

Clothing purchases

Haircuts and other salon services

Beauty products such as makeup and fragrances

Athletic gear like running shoes

Health club membership fees

Fun money (for friends and other miscellaneous gatherings)

Self-care activity money (anything you do to rejuvenate and refresh)

Hobby expenses

Children and Dependents

Childcare expenses (daycare and babysitters/nannies)

Clothing

Haircuts and other grooming costs

School supplies

School lunches

Sports and extracurricular activities

Summer camps

Toys and learning activities

Miscellaneous social/friend outings

Baby formula, diapers, and other baby costs

Allowances

Pet Care

Pet purchase fund

Pet food

Annual vet costs (check-ups, vaccinations, dewormer, etc.)

Emergency vet costs

Pet insurance (if applicable)

Training costs (if applicable)

Pet boarding/pet care costs

Grooming costs

City/county pet license costs

Other pet supplies (toys, leashes, litter supplies, etc.)

Holiday, Family, and Religion

Tithing to your local church or other religious organization

Charitable donations to causes you support

Birthday gifts

Anniversary gifts

Wedding gifts

Graduation gifts

Holiday gifts such as Easter, Christmas or Hanukkah

Bar Mitzvah, baptism, or other religious celebration gifts

Giving to your community

Social and Entertainment

Theatre, opera, and other shows

Music concerts

Day trips

Museum and Historical Society membership dues

Camping, hiking, and other nature excursions

Holiday events

Family gatherings and events

Summer gatherings such as BBQs

Friend gatherings

Sporting events (viewing)

Participatory sporting events (marathons, fun runs)

Weekend getaways

Summer vacations

Winter vacations

Debt Service other than Mortgage

Student loan payments

Credit card payments

Knowing your credit score and monitoring credit card promotions is beneficial as it informs you about various options. By staying updated with the market, you may find opportunities to transfer your outstanding balance to a different lender offering a more reasonable interest rate. Some lenders may even provide promotional introductory periods with zero percent interest options, which can be highly beneficial for credit consolidation. Considering home equity loans to reduce your interest expenses might be worthwhile if you find yourself in significant credit card debt. However, maintaining healthy spending habits is crucial to protect yourself against overwhelming debt. While unavoidable emergencies can occur, being financially responsible can help mitigate their impact.

Auto loan payments

Other personal loan payments

Repayment of loans from family

Loans for recreational vehicles

Insurance

Term Life Insurance

Auto Insurance

Health Insurance

Income Protection Insurance

Long-Term Disability Insurance

Long-Term Care Insurance (if you're age 60 or older)

Identity Theft Insurance

Business Insurance

Umbrella Policy (if you have a net worth of $500,000 or more)

Investing and Retirement

Emergency fund savings

401k savings

IRA or other retirement savings

Non-retirement investment funds

Transaction fees

Brokerage fees

Other

Upgraded house fund

Replacement car fund

Vacation fund

College savings (for yourself, your children, or your grandchildren)

Financial independence/retire early fund

Other sinking fund purposes: Managing financial obligations is crucial for maintaining a stable and secure future. Prioritizing expenses and being mindful of spending habits can help you effectively allocate resources toward debt service, insurance, investing, and other important financial goals. By carefully managing your finances, you can ensure that you make the most of your income and minimize unnecessary expenses.

One way to achieve this is by regularly monitoring your credit score. Your credit score reflects your creditworthiness and can impact your ability to secure loans or obtain favorable interest rates. By keeping an eye on your credit score, you can identify areas for improvement and take steps to build a strong credit history.

Another strategy to consider is exploring options for credit consolidation. Consolidating your debts can help you streamline your payments and reduce the overall interest expenses. This can make it easier to manage your debt and ultimately pay it off more quickly.

In addition to managing debt, it is also important to have appropriate insurance coverage. Insurance protects financially during unexpected events such as accidents, illnesses, or natural disasters. Having the right insurance policies in place can safeguard yourself and your loved ones from potential financial hardships.

Furthermore, building a solid retirement fund is essential for long-term financial security.

Planning for retirement early and consistently contributing to a retirement account can help ensure you have enough funds to support yourself in your golden years.

Making informed and responsible financial decisions can help you achieve financial stability and peace of mind. Taking the time to assess your financial situation, prioritize your expenses, and explore options for credit consolidation and insurance coverage can go a long way toward securing your financial future. Remember, it is never too early or too late to start taking control of your finances and working towards a stable and secure future.

From Penny Pinching to Financial Freedom: Unconventional Ways to Maximize Your Savings

Introduction

Let's maximize our savings accounts. Financial planning is a crucial aspect of our lives. It lays the foundation for a stable and secure future. One of the key components of financial planning is saving. Saving money not only helps us in times of emergencies but also paves the way towards financial freedom. This article will explore unconventional ways to maximize your savings beyond traditional strategies. By adopting these innovative approaches, you can take control of your finances and move closer to your goals.

Traditional savings strategies vs. unconventional savings hacks

Most people are familiar with traditional strategies for saving money, such as setting a budget, cutting back on expenses, and keeping a fixed monthly amount. While these methods are effective, there are unconventional money-saving hacks that can help you save even more.

One such hack is the "30-day rule." Instead of making impulsive purchases, wait 30 days before buying something. This helps you differentiate between wants and needs, and often, you'll find that you no longer desire the item after the waiting period.

Another unconventional savings hack is the "envelope system." Allocate a specific amount of cash for different categories of expenses and keep the money in separate envelopes. This way, your money encourages conscious consumption and helps you focus on what truly matters. Minimalism highlights your spending limits, which can help you avoid overspending. Combining traditional strategies with these unconventional hacks allows you to supercharge your savings and progress toward your financial goals faster.

The Envelope System: A Way to Stay on Top of Your Money – Stylin Spirit (stylin-spirit.com)

The wealth mindset: Shifting your perspective on saving

Saving money isn't just about restricting your spending; it's also about developing a wealth mindset, which is the belief that wealth is a mindset. A wealth mindset involves shifting your perspective on saving from scarcity to abundance. Instead of considering saving as deprivation, it can be visualized as a way to create opportunities and build wealth. Embrace the idea that you have control over your financial future and that every dollar saved brings you closer to financial freedom.

To develop a saving money mindset, start by educating yourself about personal finance. Read books, listen to podcasts, and surround yourself with like-minded individuals on the path to financial success. Additionally, practice gratitude for what you already have. By appreciating your current financial situation, you create a positive mindset that attracts more abundance into your life. Remember, developing a wealth mindset is a journey, but it can transform your financial outlook with time and effort.

Unconventional ways to maximize your savings: thinking outside the box

Thinking outside the box can lead to significant results when maximizing your savings. One unconventional way to save is by engaging in "challenge months." Challenge yourself to a month of minimal spending, where you only purchase essentials and cut out non-essential expenses. This exercise helps you save money, enables you to encourage conscious consumption, and helps you focus on what truly matters. Minimalism highlights the areas where you tend to overspend. It can be an eye-opening experience that motivates you to change your spending habits.

Another unconventional way to save is by adopting a minimalist lifestyle. Embrace the philosophy of "less is more" and declutter your life. Eliminating unnecessary possessions creates a more organized living space and saves money. Organizing your space encourages conscious consumption and helps you focus on what truly matters. By prioritizing experiences over material possessions, you can redirect your savings toward activities that bring you joy and fulfillment.

Automating your savings: Setting up systems for success

Automation is a powerful tool when it comes to maximizing your savings. By setting up systems that automatically transfer a portion of your income into a separate savings account, you eliminate the temptation to spend that money. Start by analyzing your income and expenses to determine an amount you can comfortably save each month. Then, set up an automatic transfer to ensure the designated amount goes directly into your savings account. This way, saving becomes a habit, and you won't miss the money you're putting away.

In addition to automated transfers, consider using apps and tools that help you save effortlessly. Available that track your expenses, categorize your spending, and provide insights into where you can cut costs. Numerous budgeting apps these tools can also send you reminders to save or notify you when you're overspending. By leveraging technology, you can simplify your savings process and stay on track toward your financial goals.

Cutting costs without sacrificing quality: Finding hidden savings.

There are several ways to cut costs without sacrificing the things you love. One strategy is to negotiate your bills. Contact your service providers, such as internet or cable companies, and ask for a better deal. They have promotions or discounts available that you may need to be made aware of. You can save a significant amount of money every month by simply asking.

Another way to find hidden savings is to review your subscriptions and memberships. Please review your subscribed services and assess whether they align with your current needs and priorities. Cancel any subscriptions you no longer use or find alternatives offering similar benefits at a lower cost. Regularly reviewing your subscriptions offers many advantages. By periodically reviewing your subscriptions, you can free up extra cash to be redirected towards your savings.

Leveraging technology for savings: Apps and tools to help you save

In today's digital age, technology offers several app tools and opportunities to maximize savings. Several apps and tools are specifically designed to help you save money effortlessly. One popular app is Acorns, which rounds up your purchases to the nearest dollar and invests the spare change into a diversified portfolio.

This allows you to save and invest without even thinking about it. Another helpful tool is Honey, a browser extension that automatically applies coupon codes at checkout, helping you find the best deals online.

Receipt Apps Can Help You Earn Cash and Rewards – Stylin Spirit (stylin-spirit.com)

Additionally, consider using price comparison websites and apps to ensure you get the best purchase price. These tools scan multiple online retailers and provide a list of options, allowing you to choose the most affordable one. By leveraging technology, you can become a savvy shopper and save money on everyday expenses.

Investing in your future: How to make your savings work for you

While saving money is important, making your savings work for you is equally crucial. Investing allows your money to grow over time and generate additional income. One way to start investing is by opening a retirement account, such as an Individual Retirement Account (IRA) or a 401(k). These accounts offer tax advantages and allow you to save for your future while potentially earning a higher return on your investment.

The Ultimate Showdown: 401k vs. Life Insurance as Retirement Planning Investments – Stylin Spirit (stylin-spirit.com)

Another option is to explore the world of passive income. Passive income refers to income that you earn without actively working for it. This can include rental properties, dividend-paying stocks, or even creating an online course or writing an e-book. By diversifying your income streams, you create additional sources of revenue that can contribute to your long-term financial success.

Achieving financial freedom: Setting goals and tracking progress

Setting clear goals and tracking your progress along the way is essential to achieve financial freedom. Start by defining what financial freedom means to you. Can you retire early, travel the world, or start your own business? Once you have a clear vision, break it into smaller, actionable goals. For example, if your goal is to save a certain amount for retirement, determine how much you need to save each month to reach that target.

Regularly review your finances and adjust your strategies if necessary to track your progress. Use spreadsheets or online budgeting platforms to monitor your income, expenses, and savings. Celebrate milestones along the way to stay motivated and committed to your financial journey. Remember, achieving financial freedom is a long-term process, but you can turn your dreams into reality with perseverance and dedication.

Conclusion: Embracing unconventional strategies for long-term financial success

In conclusion, traditional savings strategies can only take you so far. Embracing unconventional strategy is important to maximize your savings and achieve long-term financial success. Shift your perspective on saving by adopting a wealth mindset and thinking outside the box. Automate your savings, cut costs without sacrificing quality, and leverage technology to find hidden savings. Invest in your future and set clear goals to track your progress. By incorporating these unconventional approaches into your financial planning, you'll be on your way to transforming your financial life and achieving financial freedom.

So, why wait? Start implementing these unconventional ways to maximize your savings today and take control of your financial future!

Note: The information provided in this article is for educational purposes only and should not be considered financial advice. Please consult with a financial professional before making any investment or financial decisions.

Credit Scores Explained: Why They Matter and How They Work

Credit scores stand at the forefront of financial health, influencing decisions beyond simple loan approvals and interest rates. These numerical expressions are pivotal for insurers, landlords, and even cell phone providers, dictating terms for premiums, rentals, and plan agreements. As cornerstones in the vast financial landscape, credit scores encapsulate an individual's fiscal reliability, affecting access to mortgages, personal loans, student loans, and credit card agreements. Their profound impact extends to determining mortgage rates and safeguarding against potential defaults and bankruptcies, underscoring their indispensability in modern financial management.

Navigating the complexities of credit scores involves understanding their calculation, the major models such as the FICO score, and the diverse credit score ranges recommended for financial stability. This article demystifies the mechanics behind credit scores, outlines steps for credit repair, and explores the instrumental role of credit bureaus and reports. By arming readers with knowledge on how to enhance their credit ratings and manage credit card debt and credit lines effectively, it aims to foster financial empowerment and smarter lending practices among individuals striving for economic resilience.

hat Is a Credit Score?

The credit score is at the heart of financial health and decision-making, a three-digit number that calculates an individual's creditworthiness. This score, which in the U.S. ranges from 300 to 850, encapsulates an individual's ability to manage and repay borrowed money responsibly. Understanding what constitutes a credit score must be balanced, as it influences the availability of credit and the terms under which credit is offered.

Credit Score Ranges and Their Meaning:

Poor Credit: 300-579

Fair Credit: 580-669

Good Credit: 670-739

Very Good Credit: 740-799

Excellent Credit: 800-850

These categories, as defined by the FICO scoring model, help lenders quickly assess an applicant's credit risk. Higher scores indicate a lower risk to lenders, often resulting in more favorable credit terms, including lower interest rates and higher credit limits.

Factors influencing credit scores are diverse and include:

Repayment History: Timeliness of past payments.

Credit Utilization: Ratio of current revolving credit (e.g., credit card balances) to the total available revolving credit.

Length of Credit History: The duration for which one has maintained credit accounts.

Types of Credit: The mix of account types, such as credit cards, mortgage loans, and personal loans.

New Credit: The number of recently opened credit accounts and credit inquiries.

It's crucial to note what factors do not influence credit scores. Personal information such as race, religion, nationality, gender, marital status, and employment details are excluded from credit score calculations. This ensures that the score fairly represents an individual's credit behavior rather than their personal characteristics or life situation.

Understanding credit scores is foundational to navigating the financial landscape. Whether applying for a mortgage, a credit card, or a personal loan, the credit score plays a pivotal role in determining the terms of credit offered. Companies rely on these scores to predict credit behavior, such as the likelihood of repaying a loan on time, making them a critical tool in financial decision-making processes.

The Major Credit Score Models

Two primary models stand out in the realm of credit scores due to their widespread use and influence on lending decisions: the FICO score and VantageScore. Each model has its unique approach to evaluating creditworthiness, though they share the common goal of providing lenders with a reliable metric to assess lending risk.

FICO Score:

Usage: Over 90% of top lenders adopted it, making it the most influential credit score model.

Range: Scores span from 300 to 850, where scores under 600 are deemed poor, and those above 740 are considered excellent.

Variations for Specific Purposes: FICO offers different types of scores tailored for particular financial products, including auto loans and credit cards.

Categories: Scores are divided into poor (300-599), fair (600-649), good (650-699), very good (700-749), and excellent (750-850).VantageScore:

Creation: Developed collaboratively by the three major credit bureaus—Equifax, Experian, and TransUnion.

Range: Also ranges from 300 to 850, aligning with the FICO score range for consistency across models.

Innovations: The VantageScore 4.0 model utilizes trended data, offering insights into how a borrower's credit behavior changes over time.

Credit Bureaus' Models: Each of the three bureaus also maintains its proprietary scoring models, further diversifying the credit scoring landscape.

A pivotal aspect of understanding credit scores is recognizing that they can vary significantly depending on several factors. These include the requesting company, the type of business inquiring about the score, and the specific credit reporting bureau and scoring model used. This variation underscores the complex nature of credit scoring and the importance of maintaining a healthy financial profile across different dimensions. Additionally, the secretive nature of scoring model algorithms—closely guarded by the companies that develop them—adds a layer of mystery to how scores are precisely calculated. However, the primary factors influencing scores are well-documented and consistent across models.

Given the diversity in scoring models and the potential for variance in scores, individuals are encouraged to monitor their credit through various channels. Understanding that different lenders might use different bureaus and models can help anticipate discrepancies in reported scores. This knowledge empowers consumers to engage more effectively with their financial health, striving for improvement and clarity in their credit profiles.

How Credit Scores Are Calculated

Understanding the intricate process of how credit scores are calculated is fundamental in navigating the financial landscape. The calculation is based on a complex algorithm that considers various elements of an individual's financial history, each carrying a different weight. Here's a breakdown of these components:

Payment History (35% for FICO, 40% for VantageScore)

This is the most critical factor, reflecting how timely an individual has been with their payments. Late payments can severely damage credit scores, more so the longer a payment is overdue.

Components such as late payments, bankruptcies, and collections fall under this category, emphasizing the importance of maintaining a consistent payment schedule.

Amounts Owed/Credit Utilization (30% for FICO, 20% for VantageScore)

This measures the ratio of current revolving credit (like credit card balances) against the total available credit. A lower ratio is better, with keeping utilization below about 10% being ideal for boosting scores.

High utilization signals a higher risk of default to lenders, negatively impacting credit scores.

Length of Credit History (15% for FICO, 21% for VantageScore)

A more extended credit history typically results in higher scores, as it provides more data on an individual's financial behavior over time.

The age of the oldest account and the average age of all accounts are considered, highlighting the benefit of maintaining long-standing credit accounts.

Credit Mix (10% for FICO)

Having various credit types (e.g., mortgage, car loans, credit cards) can positively influence credit scores, showing that an individual can manage different types of credit responsibly.

New Credit (10% for FICO)

Applying for several new credit lines in a short period can be risky, particularly for those with short credit histories. It's crucial to space out credit applications to minimize their impact on credit scores.

Additional Considerations:

Self-checks or soft inquiries on credit scores do not affect the score, allowing individuals to monitor their credit without penalty.

Rent and utility payments are generally not included in credit score calculations unless reported due to late payments or through a rent-reporting service.

Factors like income, bank balances, and age do not directly impact credit scores, though they may indirectly influence an individual's ability to secure credit.

By understanding these components and their significance in calculating credit scores, individuals can take informed steps toward managing their financial profiles more effectively.

The Impact of Your Credit Score

The significance of credit scores transcends mere numbers, shaping the financial landscape of opportunities and challenges individuals face. These scores, pivotal in financial decision-making, impact various aspects of one's financial life in profound ways:

Loan and Credit Opportunities:

Credit Cards and Loans: A robust credit score enhances eligibility for a broader range of credit cards and loans, often with more attractive terms.

Interest Rates: Higher scores typically secure lower interest rates, translating to considerable savings over time. For instance, a high credit score can reduce interest payments by thousands on mortgages and auto loans.

Approval Odds: Lenders view higher scores as indicative of lower risk, increasing the likelihood of loan and credit approval.

Housing and Utilities:

Renting: Landlords often check credit scores to gauge potential tenants' reliability. A higher score can simplify the rental process and expand housing options.

Utilities: Some utility companies require deposits for new accounts, but a good credit score might waive these deposits, easing initial setup costs.

Insurance and Employment:

Insurance Premiums: Insurers may use credit scores to determine auto and homeowners insurance premiums, with better scores potentially leading to lower premiums.

Job Opportunities: Certain employers review credit scores as part of the hiring process, particularly for roles involving financial responsibilities.

Financial Savings and Benefits:

Mortgages: The impact of credit scores on mortgage rates is stark. A high score (760-850) could secure a rate of 3.307% on a $200,000, 30-year mortgage, while a lower score (620-639) might result in a rate of 4.869%, costing an additional $66,343 over the loan's lifetime.

Auto Loans: For An excellent credit score for a 5-year, $41,000 auto loan saves approximately $3,251 in interest compared to lower scores.

Personal Loans: A good credit score can also lead to savings on personal loans, with a potential $885 saved in interest on a 3-year, $10,000 loan.

These examples underscore the tangible benefits of maintaining a good credit score, from easing the path to homeownership and vehicle financing to mitigating costs associated with insurance and utility services. One's credit score significantly influences the journey toward financial stability and freedom, highlighting the importance of credit management and monitoring.

Improving Your Credit Score: Step-by-Step

Improving your credit score is a journey that requires patience, discipline, and a strategic approach. Here are key steps to follow:

Timely Payments:

Automate Payments: Setting up automatic payments for bills ensures you never miss a due date, directly influencing your payment history positively.

Due-Date Alerts: For accounts where automation isn't possible or preferred, setting up due-date alerts can serve as a helpful reminder.

Credit Utilization Management:

Keep Balances Low: Aim to keep your credit card balances well below their limits. A rule of thumb is maintaining a credit utilization rate of 30% or less.

Request Credit Limit Increases: Without increasing your spending, higher credit limits can automatically lower your utilization rate.

Credit Mix and New Credit:

Diverse Credit Portfolio: Having a mix of credit types (credit cards, personal loans, student loans) can positively impact your score. However, it's crucial to manage them responsibly.

Limit New Applications: Each new credit application can result in a hard inquiry, which might negatively affect your score. Space out credit applications and only apply for what you truly need.

Additional Strategies:

Review Credit Reports: Regularly checking your credit reports from all three major credit bureaus (Equifax, Experian, TransUnion) can help you identify and dispute any inaccuracies, potentially improving your credit score.

Address Past-Due Accounts: Catching up on past-due accounts stops them from further harming your score and might also persuade creditors to report them more favorably.

Consider Credit-Building Tools: Services like Experian Boost or UltraFICO can factor in alternative data, such as utility payments, potentially benefitting your credit score.

Maintain Old Accounts: The age of your credit accounts contributes to your credit score. Keep older accounts open and in good standing to benefit from a longer credit history.

By adopting these strategies, individuals can work towards improving their credit scores, unlocking the door to financial opportunities and savings. Remember, credit scores are dynamic and can change based on your financial behaviors. Consistent application of these practices can lead to significant improvements over time, reflecting positively on your financial health and stability.

Understanding Your Credit Report

Understanding the intricacies of your credit report is paramount in maintaining a healthy financial profile. A credit report is essentially a detailed record of an individual's financial behavior, encompassing various elements that collectively influence their credit score. Here's a breakdown of the key components found in a credit report:

Personal Information: Includes the individual's name, Social Security number, birth date, current and previous addresses, and contact information. Ensuring this information is accurate is crucial for identity verification and preventing errors or fraud.

Employer History: Lists current and past employers, which lenders can use to set status and stability.

Credit History:

Accounts from the past seven to ten years, both current and closed.

Types of accounts (revolving credit, installment loans).

Payment history, including late or missed payments.

Current balances, credit limits or loan amounts, and account status (e.g., active, closed, default).

Names of creditors and lenders, along with account opening and closing dates.

Public Records: Bankruptcies, foreclosures, and repossessions are included here, significantly impacting credit scores.

Credit Inquiries: Distinguishes between soft inquiries (which do not affect credit scores) and hard inquiries (which may lower scores by a few points).

Regular monitoring of your credit report is essential for several reasons:

Accuracy Check: Reviewing your credit report regularly helps ensure all listed information is accurate. If discrepancies are found, promptly contacting the lender or credit bureau for correction is vital.

Detecting Errors and Identity Theft: Early detection of unauthorized activities or errors can prevent them from negatively affecting your credit score.

Understanding Credit Health: Knowing what factors currently influence your credit score can guide you in making informed financial decisions.

Lenders update Credit reports monthly, providing a dynamic overview of an individual's financial status. Individuals are entitled to one free copy of their credit report annually from each of the three major credit reporting agencies. This accessibility empowers individuals to take charge of their financial health by staying informed about their credit status.

It's important to note that while employers can access a modified version of your credit report, they cannot see your credit score. Additionally, certain aspects like parking tickets and library fines do not appear on credit reports, though they may indirectly impact financial health if left unpaid. Understanding these nuances is crucial in navigating the complexities of credit reports and their role in financial well-being.

Common Misconceptions About Credit Scores

Navigating the landscape of credit scores involves dispelling common misconceptions that can cloud one's understanding of how they work and impact financial health. Here, we address prevalent myths with factual clarifications to foster a deeper comprehension of credit dynamics.

Soft Inquiries vs. Hard Inquiries:

Myth: Checking your own credit score lowers it.

Fact: Checking your own credit score is a soft inquiry and does not impact your score. It's essential for monitoring credit health.

Credit Card Balances:

Myth: Carrying a balance on your credit card boosts your credit score.

Fact: Paying off your balance in full each month is recommended. Carrying a balance does not improve your score and incurs interest.

Income and Wealth:

Myth: A high income or wealth equates to a good credit score.

Fact: Income does not impact your credit score. Responsible credit management reflects in your score, irrespective of income levels.

Effects of Marriage and Debit Card Use:

Marriage: Your credit scores remain independent post-marriage. Each individual maintains their own report and score.

Debit Card Use: Transactions with a debit card, including selecting 'credit' at checkout, do not influence your credit score.

Closing Credit Cards:

Myth: Closing a credit card does not impact your credit score.

Fact: Closing a credit card can affect your credit utilization ratio and shorten your credit history, potentially lowering your score.

Credit Score Variances:

Myth: There is a one-size-fits-all approach to credit scores and reports.

Fact: Credit reports and scores vary by individual, reflecting unique financial behaviors and histories.

Credit Application Impacts:

Myth: Applying for new credit drastically lowers your FICO Score.

Fact: While new credit applications can cause a slight dip, this is typically minor, especially for auto or mortgage loans applied for within a short timeframe.

Credit Scoring Fairness:

Myth: Credit scoring considers personal factors like gender, race, or marital status.

Fact: Credit scoring is based solely on financial behaviors and does not account for personal characteristics, ensuring fairness.

By confronting these myths with truths, individuals can confidently navigate their financial journeys, understanding that credit scores reflect credit management practices rather than personal attributes or life circumstances. This knowledge empowers consumers to take proactive steps in maintaining or improving their credit scores, ultimately unlocking opportunities for financial growth and stability.

Credit Score Monitoring and Management Tools

In the quest to maintain and enhance credit scores, individuals have a variety of credit monitoring and management tools at their disposal. These tools assist in tracking credit progress and Experian credit reports and offer actionable insights for improvement. Here's a closer look at some notable services:

Aura:

Features: Combines identity theft protection, three-bureau credit monitoring, digital security tools, and up to $5 million in identity theft insurance for family plans.

Support: Offers 24/7 U.S.-based support.

Experian:

Free Services: Access to FICO credit score, Experian credit report, and Experian Boost for potential score improvement.

Premium Membership: Includes credit score comparison, subscription cancellation and bill negotiation service, identity theft insurance, fraud alerts, and resolution support.

Credit Karma:

Access: Free access to Equifax and TransUnion credit scores and reports.

Features: Weekly updates, insights on factors affecting credit score, financial calculators, and credit product matching.

Utilizing these tools effectively requires regular engagement and a proactive stance toward credit management. By staying informed and responsive to changes in their credit reports, individuals can confidently navigate the complexities of credit scores, ensuring their financial well-being.

Conclusion

Understanding and managing one's credit score is essential to financial health, bridging the gap between current financial standing and future financial opportunities. Throughout this article, we've explored the nuances of credit scores, from their calculation and impact to strategies for improvement and the power of vigilant monitoring. The journey towards financial resilience is marked by informed decisions and careful management of credit activities, underlining the importance of credit scores in securing favorable financial terms and broadening access to essential financial resources.

As individuals arm themselves with the knowledge of how credit scores operate and their significant impact on various facets of financial well-being, it becomes evident that proactive engagement with one's credit health can open doors to financial freedom and stability. By debunking common myths, understanding credit reports, and utilizing available tools for monitoring and improvement, consumers are better positioned to navigate the financial landscape. Thus, embracing the principles laid out in this exploration of credit scores is a pivotal step toward achieving and maintaining financial empowerment and resilience.

www.ingramcontent.com/pod-product-compliance
Lightning Source LLC
Chambersburg PA
CBHW071832210526
45479CB00001B/106